Peer Mediation Training

for Key Stages 1, 2 and 3

Hilary Stacey

Lucky Duck is more than a publishing house and training agency. George Robinson and Barbara Maines founded the company in the 1980s when they worked together as a head and psychologist developing innovative strategies to support challenging students.

They have an international reputation for their work on bullying, self-esteem, emotional literacy and many other subjects of interest to the world of education.

George and Barbara have set up a regular news-spot on the website. Twice yearly these items will be printed as a newsletter. If you would like to go on the mailing list to receive this then please contact us:

e-mail newsletter@luckyduck.co.uk website www.luckyduck.co.uk

ISBN: 1 873 942 58 3

Published by Lucky Duck Publishing Ltd

www.luckyduck.co.uk

Reprinted May 2004

Acknowledgements

This video and handbook include many ideas that Pat Robinson developed over her five year involvement with Catalyst. In particular, I would like to thank Pat for the Peer Assessment forms and the Mediator's script that can be found in this handbook.

I would like to acknowledge Pat's inspiration, intelligence and generosity, without which this video and handbook would be much the poorer.

I would also like to acknowledge Liz Rance's input into Section Two of the handbook, and the tireless efforts of Sue and Di to keep Catalyst running smoothly.

Huge thanks to Daniel Cremin for his creative ideas and daily on-going support in more ways than I could mention.

Foreword

The video, manual and the publication *Let's Mediate* provide a comprehensive series of training sessions to support the teaching of mediation skills to primary and secondary aged students. Staff using the material will be able to work with young people from the first introduction through the teaching of the skills to the maintenance of the system once established.

The programme has been produced with Catalyst Consultancy - a training organisation which has a long experience of teaching young people in schools and supporting staff in the implementation of Peer Mediation initiatives.

The structure of the programme has four stages:

1. Introduction to Peer Mediation
2. Laying the foundations for Peer Mediation
3. Selecting the mediators and organising the training
4. A programme of Peer Mediation using the video.

Contents

Section One

Introduction to Peer Mediation

What is mediation?

Mediation is, "A structured process in which a neutral third party assists voluntary participants in their dispute." Stacey and Robinson (1997) *Let's Mediate.*

Mediation is NOT:

- about deciding who is 'right' or 'wrong'
- apportioning blame
- about focusing on the past any more than is necessary to help the disputants to work out the way forward in the future.

Mediators do NOT offer advice. Instead, they support disputants to find mutually acceptable solutions.

Mediation allows disputants to:

- define the 'problem', from their point of view
- identify and express their feelings and needs
- hear the feelings and needs of the other person
- acknowledge each other's point of view
- create solutions
- agree a course of action
- evaluate progress, and repeat if necessary
- to explore the mediation process.

Apart from in schools, mediation is used in a range of other contexts. Mediation is obviously used in international disputes, but it is also used to resolve issues in divorce proceedings, and in industry and commerce to resolve contractual disputes and to avoid costly litigation. Uses of mediation in the community include mediation through housing departments to resolve neighbour disputes, and through probation and juvenile justice to offer victim-offender reparation.

Mediation is relatively new in the UK. It started in the USA during the 1970s and

1980s. President Jimmy Carter encouraged establishment of first Neighbourhood Justice Centres where mediation was used to provide alternative to court proceedings. The success of early US projects both in the community and in schools was impressive, and the 1980s and 1990s saw significant growth of the concept of mediation internationally across a wide range of organisations.

The key principles in mediation are that:

- mediators do not offer solutions
- mediation is not counselling...it's task orientated
- mediators do not make judgements of any kind
- mediation is a voluntary process
- disputants attack the problem and not each other.

Peer Mediation in Schools

The 'peer' in Peer Mediation can either refer to a small number of pupils within a year group trained to offer a service to others of the same age, or to older pupils mediating younger pupils throughout the school. It can also refer to a team made up of pupils drawn from across the year groups.

Pupils will normally have covered foundation work in conflict resolution and have had an introduction to the mediation process before they nominate themselves or others for further training which takes place off-timetable over three days. An intensive period of time such as this allows for team building, proper rehearsal of counselling skills and for the pupils to develop their own guidelines for effective practice. Included in this training are the members of staff who will support the peer mediators throughout the year, lunchtime supervisors, and any other adults or ancillary staff offering their support (Education Social Workers, School Nurse, Secretarial staff, parents, governors or home/school liaison workers). Although peer mediators have ownership of their service and make decisions about the way in which the service runs, they also have regular adult support and supervision. This support varies according to the age of the pupils involved, but all have a weekly team meeting to debrief, to share experiences, and to keep up a regular programme of review and development.

When the services are initially set up, decisions are made about what sorts of problems are appropriate for pupil mediators to deal with and how pupils access the service. The finer details of rota and responsibilities for running the scheme from day to day are also considered. In many models, the service takes place at lunchtime four times a week. Some choose to withdraw into a quiet room or private corner, whilst other services operate out in play areas at a designated spot. Peer Mediation services are more likely to be well used when a high profile is maintained throughout the school year. In many of these successful initiatives teams of mediators gave themselves a clear identity, choosing names (Trouble Busters, Helping Hands, and Untanglers) logos, slogans ('Release the peace and be strong') and forms of identification such as baseball caps, badges and sweatshirts.

The usual stage at which pupils are trained to become peer mediators is at top junior level or secondary level. It is, however, possible to train KS1 mediators using a simplified version of the mediation process. Infants mediate in the sense that they can support two people in disagreement to hear each other's feelings and agree what to do for the best. Juniors, however, are able to provide a neutral, non-judgemental service in which they can help disputants to understand what the problem is about, appreciate each others point of view, and choose a way forward. Secondary pupils use their growing maturity, perception, and sophistication, to reach underlying issues as well as to identify unexpressed needs. A mediation between primary pupils may be over in a matter of minutes. Older pupils may need recourse to several sessions of mediation before reaching a resolution to their dispute.

What benefits can it bring?

Hilary Cremin's Ph.D. research, available from University College, Northampton, UK, evaluated the effectiveness of a Peer Mediation programme in three primary schools in Birmingham. A quasi-experiment, involving pupil questionnaires and teacher interviews, was used to measure changes in levels of bullying, and levels of pupil self-esteem and locus of control, following Peer Mediation training of Year 5 and the setting up of a Peer Mediation scheme.

In School One the Peer Mediation Programme coincided with the following changes:

- there was a reduction in the frequency of pupils reporting being a victim of bullying
- there was a reduction in the frequency of pupils reporting bullying others
- types of bullying that appeared to reduce were physical bullying, teasing and psychological bullying
- pupil self-esteem improved after an initial dip, which suggests that pupils were undergoing some far-reaching reassessment of their self-concepts
- pupil feelings of empowerment improved
- pupils developed more negative attitudes towards bullying
- after the Peer Mediation training programme, pupils had improved their ability to resolve conflicts, to give and receive positive comments, to co-operate, to communicate, and to listen to each other. By the time the Peer

Mediation scheme had been running for two terms, they were beginning to transfer these skills to situations outside of the classroom, and many pupils had developed a high level of competency in these areas
- pupils with emotional and behavioural difficulties appeared to gain a great deal from this approach, with all pupils benefiting from a general reduction in disaffection and aggressive behaviour.

In this school, there was a whole-school approach with extensive staff training. The programme built on a negotiated, well-established, code of conduct and reward system, and pupils were consulted about decisions that would affect their daily lives in many different ways. The headteacher and teachers appeared keen to hear about, and act on, instances of bullying, and modelled the mediation process themselves in their dealings with conflict in the classroom and playground. Pupils were able to practice personal, social and conflict resolution skills in real situations, and this led to a positive school culture. In particular, the headteacher had realistically assessed the starting points and training needs of the pupils and staff.

In the other two schools, no Peer Mediation service was set up following the Peer Mediation training, and there were no apparent changes in pupil levels of bullying, self-esteem and locus of control. In these two schools, the programme was limited to Year 5 and the headteachers appeared to over-estimate the skill level of their staff in solving conflicts without confrontation. It also appeared that pupils were sometimes discouraged from talking about bullying, with victims ignored or blamed by some teachers. Structured lessons, teacher control, and playground supervision were used as anti-bullying strategies, and negative behaviour was at times excused on the grounds of supposed lack of parental skill and support. The code of conduct and reward schemes were still being formulated in both schools.

How can it be implemented as part of a whole-school initiative?

Some of the elements of a whole-school approach are discussed above. In essence, the Peer Mediation service needs to be part of a wider initiative to improve responses to conflict in school. This wider approach needs to involve both adults and children in the school community. If Peer Mediation is seen as a 'bolt-on' to life in school, or if adults in school undermine the use of non-adversarial approaches to conflict through aggression or confrontation, then the benefits will be short lived.

The following tables provide a model for introducing mediation training into primary and secondary schools.

Primary School Project Outline

Key Outcomes:

- Whole staff training in Circle Time to teach social and emotional conflict resolution skills to all pupils through PSHE from the nursery upwards
- A trained peer mediation co-ordinator
- Peer Mediation training for Year 5 pupils
- Lunchtime supervisors and parent training in mediation techniques.

Term 1	
Initial consultation	Senior and middle managers and prospective peer mediation coordinator
Peer mediation co-ordinator training - 2 days	Peer mediation co-ordinator
Teacher day on Circle Time to teach core social, emotional and conflict resolution skills through PSHE	All staff
Term 2	
Circle Time is introduced in all classes	All staff supported by peer mediation co-ordinator
Training in mediation techniques - 2 days	Lunchtime supervisors, parents, others
Peer mediators are selected and trained	Peer mediation co-ordinator and 16 - 20 Year 5 pupils
Peer mediation service is set up	Peer mediators and peer mediation co-ordinator
Term 3	
Peer mediation service runs	Peer mediators and peer mediation co-ordinator
After school review meeting	All staff

Secondary School Project Outline

Key Outcomes

- Whole staff training including lunchtime supervisors to clarify aims and objectives for the project
- Focussed staff training and tailor-written PSHE materials for all tutors in the target year group
- All pupils in the year group to receive some training in the skills underpinning mediation
- Peer mediation training for a team of mediators
- A peer mediation service for that year group with possibility of extension
- Lunchtime supervisors and parent training in mediation techniques.

Term 1	
Initial consultation	Senior and middle managers and prospective peer mediation co-ordinator(s)
After school information meeting	All staff
Training in techniques to teach social, emotional and conflict resolution skills through PSHE - 2 days	The tutor team of the target year group e.g. next years Year 8 tutor team
Planning a half term PSHE programme as above	Year head, PSHE co-ordinator and peer mediation co-ordinator
Term 2	
PSHE programme for all pupils - 8 weeks	Tutor team
Training in mediation techniques - 2 days	Peer mediation co-ordinator(s), lunchtime supervisors, parents, others
Assembly to introduce peer mediation to pupils and recruit mediators	Peer mediators from another school and target year group
Peer mediation training - 3 days	16 pupils from target year group, peer mediation co-ordinator(s) and others
Peer mediation service is set up	Peer mediation co-ordinator(s) and tutors
Term 3	
Peer mediation service runs	Peer mediation co-ordinator(s) and tutors
Review meeting	Peer mediation co-ordinator(s) and tutors

Many staff think, quite justifiably, that there is an 'initiative overdrive' within the current education system. Although this makes the introduction of yet another whole-school initiative problematic, an argument can be made that a Peer Mediation system properly set up and run can save staff time in the long run. In addition to this, an argument can also be made that Circle Time and Peer Mediation are ideal vehicles for the delivery of PSHE through Curriculum 2000.

Section Two

Laying the foundations for Peer Mediation

The 30 minute whole-staff briefing based on the video

The following 4 OHT's can be used with the video for a 30 minute presentation for staff. The presentation can be based on Section One of this handbook. A typical briefing session could take the following format:

1. Show OHT 1 and discuss the aims of this session.
2. Ask staff to discuss between themselves what they already know about mediation. Brainstorm onto a flipchart.
3. Show OHT 2 and suggest this as a definition of mediation.
4. Use OHT 3 as a basis for discussing the stages of mediation.
5. Use OHT 4 to discuss the aims of teaching mediation in schools. Widen the discussion to talk about what benefits the staff in your school might expect, and how they might contribute to the success of the scheme.
6. Show the pupils mediating in Section 2 of the video. You may also want to show the peer mediators and teachers reflecting on the use of Peer Mediation in their schools in Section 4 of the video.

Aims of this session:

- to consider what mediation is

- to explore the mediation process

- to watch pupils mediating and discuss how Peer Mediation works.

OHT 1

What is mediation?

"A structured process in which a neutral third party assists voluntary participants in resolving their dispute."

Stacey and Robinson, 1997, Let's Mediate.

OHT 2

What does mediation allow disputants to do?

- define the problem from their point of view
- identify and express their feelings and needs
- hear the feelings and needs of the of the other person
- acknowledge each other's point of view
- create solutions
- agree a course of action
- evaluate progress, and repeat if necessary.

OHT 3

The aims of teaching mediation in schools:

- to develop social skills for pupils and staff in dealing with conflict in a more positive way
- to create a calm, co-operative classroom atmosphere
- to affirm pupils and raise their self esteem
- to give pupils alternatives to disruption and violence
- to create understanding and awareness of others
- to give pupils ownership of their own resolution of disputes
- to enhance learning through creating a safer, more positive environment.

(Birmingham teachers,1993)

OHT 4

Using Let's Mediate to deliver a ten-hour preliminary Circle Time and conflict resolution course through PSHE

In order for the Peer Mediation service to be successful, pupils will need to do some groundwork. Both mediators and the pupils who will be using the service will need fairly well developed speaking, listening, co-operation and problem-solving skills. This work can be started through PSHE and Circle Time, and consolidated once the pupils are actually using the service.

The publication *Let's Mediate* contains a wealth of ideas for teaching these core personal and social skills, but the following planning document may be useful as a starting point for teachers of pupils who are new to this way of working. It will need to be adapted for the age of the pupils, and to reflect the pupil's existing level of skill. The document assumes a mixed ability class of upper primary or lower secondary pupils, and is for ten 30 minute sessions. Ideally each session should be repeated and extended at least once.

Session One: Introducing Circle Time

The video *Coming Round to Circle Time* and the introductory books, *Circle Time* and *Developing Circle Time* provide and excellent resource for increasing the confidence of teachers wanting to introduce Circle Time for the first time or those who have made a start but are looking for new ideas to extend the activities. All the resources are available from Lucky Duck Publishing Ltd.

Aims

- To introduce the rules and conventions of Circle Time.
- To negotiate the ground rules for these sessions.
- To improve speaking and listening skills.
- To find out more about each other and stress commonality.
- To generate an atmosphere of fun.

Content

(Each of these activities is described in *Let's Mediate* - Page numbers are referenced.)

1. Get the pupils into a circle of chairs with nothing in the middle of the circle.
   Let's Mediate p 18 and 38.
   Discuss and agree the rules for Circle Time. The following are typical:
   - Only talk when you are holding the talking object
   - Treat what anyone says with respect and don't laugh at anyone or contradict him or her
   - You have the right to pass.

2. Use a soft ball that is easy to catch to play the 'First Introductions' game.
   Let's Mediate p 27.

3. Play the 'Introducing Partners Round the Circle' game.
   Let's Mediate p 27.

4. Do a go-round; e.g. 'I like to…' (for a leisure activity).
   Let's Mediate p 46.
   Everyone should contribute, and anyone who passes can be given another go at the end. Those who have poor speaking skills should not be put under undue pressure, and those with poor listening skills should be reminded firmly of the ground rules. Keep the pace fast, and try not to exceed the attention span of your pupils.

5. Play 'I Love All my Friends' as a mixing and energising game.
   Let's Mediate p 31.

6. Pair the pupils off around the circle (stress that in Circle Time everyone needs to be able to work with anyone in the class, and it is unacceptable to moan about who your partner is). Give them 2 minutes to find two things that they both enjoy doing, and then share one each with the rest of the group.
   Let's Mediate p 47-49.

7. Final game, e.g. 'Fives'.
   Let's Mediate p 95.

Session Two: More Circle Time

Aims

- To consolidate the rules and conventions of Circle Time.
- To strengthen the quality of peer relationships.
- To strengthen speaking and listening skills.
- To enhance memory.

Content

Remind everyone of the rules.

1. Play 'I Love All my Friends' to mix pupils up and improve concentration skills.
   Let's Mediate p 31.

2. Ask the pupils to tell their partner three things about themselves. They then tell the rest of the group the three things they can remember about their partner.
   Let's Mediate p 47.

3. Play a game, e.g. 'Spontaneous Counting'.
   Let's Mediate p 95.

4. Do a go-round, e.g. 'One thing I love is... and one thing I hate is...'
   Let's Mediate p 46.

5. Use 'Listening Checks' to show how important it is to really listen and remember things about other people.
   Let's Mediate p 49.

6. Play a game, e.g. 'Fives'.
   Let's Mediate p 95.

Session Three: Co-operation skills

Aims

- To consolidate the rules and conventions of Circle Time.
- To strengthen the quality of peer relationships.
- To improve pupils' co-operation skills in the context of a game.

Content

(If you have a parachute in school, you may want to use it in a PE lesson to teach these skills. See *Let's Mediate* p 86-88 and 91)

1. Get the pupils into a circle of chairs. Play one of the games that they already know. Let them choose. Discuss how they made sure that the choice was fair.

2. Play 'Rainforest'. Extend with a circle music activity?
   Let's Mediate p 89.

3. Do a go-round where they say the ways that they co-operate with other people.
   Let's Mediate p 46.

4. Play 'Silent Ordering'. Discuss how well they co-operated.
   Let's Mediate p 93.

5. Play a co-operative game, e.g. 'Co-operative Knots'.
   Let's Mediate p 94-95.

Session Four: More co-operation skills

Aims

- To encourage pupils to reflect on the value of co-operation.
- To encourage pupils to be more aware of their own ability to co-operate.

Content

1. With pupils sitting in small groups around tables, play and discuss 'Co-operative Pictures'.
   Let's Mediate p 93.

2. Either:

a) Go to the hall or the playground and play some PE type co-operative games, e.g. 'Sitting on Laps', ***Let's Mediate p 96*** and 'Co-operative Bodywork', ***Let's Mediate p 96.***

or

b) Play and discuss 'Co-operative Goodies'.
Let's Mediate p 91.
The most valuable aspect of all of these activities is a careful and reflective discussion and analysis of individual pupil's responses to situations where they were required to co-operate.

Session Five: Improving Self-esteem

Aims

- To improve the self-esteem of the pupils.
- To provide vocabulary and ideas for giving compliments.
- To begin to explore the hurtful nature of name-calling.

Content

1. Do a brainstorming activity to record as many positive adjectives, personal qualities and abilities as possible.
   Let's Mediate p 67.

2. Use the 'Fruit Bowl' idea to get the pupils to share one positive thing about themselves with the others.
   Let's Mediate p 78.

3. Do the first part of the 'How name calling hurts us' activity.
   Let's Mediate p 82.

4. Set the class a challenge of not calling each other names for an identified period of time.
   Let's Mediate p 74.

Session Six: More improving Self-esteem

Aims

- To improve the self-esteem of the pupils.
- To support pupils to accept positive feedback about themselves.
- To further explore the hurtful nature of name-calling.

Content

1. Get pupils into a circle of chairs. Play 'I Love All my Friends...' to mix pupils up and improve concentration skills. Use things they are good at as a theme for the game.
   Let's Mediate p 31.

2. Get the pupils into pairs around the circle and ask them to tell their partner one thing they are good at. The partners then feed this back to the group for each other.
   Let's Mediate p 75.

3. Do 'Fame for the Day' with one emotionally mature pupil. Ideally this activity will be continued with everyone chosen at random on a weekly basis.
   Let's Mediate p 79.

4. Do the second part of the 'How name calling hurts us' activity.
   Let's Mediate p 82.

5. Evaluate how they did in the class challenge of not calling each other names for an identified period of time.
   Let's Mediate p 74.

Session Seven: Emotional Intelligence

Aims

- To improve pupils' feelings vocabulary.
- To help pupils' become more aware of their feelings.

Content

1. Use the 'Feelings Wall' activity to brainstorm and write up a wide range of feelings. Over the coming week, get pupils to periodically point to their feelings on the feelings wall.
   Let's Mediate p 109.

2. Get the pupils into a circle. Play 'Guess my Feeling', 'Pass the Face' and 'Sentence Completion' for Expressing Feelings.
   Let's Mediate p 106-108.

Session Eight: More Emotional Intelligence

Aims

- To help pupils' become more aware of their feelings.
- To help pupils' reach a better understanding of what happens when they get angry and how to control angry impulses.

Content

1. Get the pupils into a circle. Play any warm-up game that the pupils enjoy.

2. Do the 'One to Ten' activity with the pupils.
   Let's Mediate p 112.

3. Do the 'How Feelings Affect' us activity, using anger as the feeling, either in the circle or in small groups feeding back to the circle.
   Let's Mediate p 115.

4. Use the 'Red Flags' worksheet (filled out earlier?) to stimulate discussion about what makes pupils feel angry, and how they manage to control angry impulses.
   Let's Mediate p 135.

5. Play an active game to work off any residual angry feelings that have been brought to the surface during these activities!

Session Nine: Understanding different perspectives

Aims

- To encourage an awareness that others may have different experiences, interests and perspectives.
- To strengthen pupils' tolerance of others.

Content

1. Use the 'Picture It' activity to discuss the ways that people organise information differently depending on their perspectives and interests.
   Let's Mediate p 152.

2. Either:

a) Do the 'Ideal Enemies activity to explore how people project things that they don't like about themselves onto other people.
Let's Mediate p 136.

or

b) Use the 'Red and Blue realities' activity to discuss how people jump to conclusions based on limited information about others.
Let's Mediate p 153.

Session Ten: Problem Solving

Aims

- To explore the difference between brainstorming and evaluating with the pupils.
- To teach about different conflict styles and encourage pupils to have a wider range of conflict resolution strategies available to them.

Content

1. Use the 'Brainstorming and Evaluating' activity to teach pupils the difference between these two ways of thinking.
   Let's Mediate p 154.

2. Do the 'Fist and Palm' exercise and the 'Conflict Questionnaire' to stimulate discussion about how people respond differently to conflict situations.
   Let's Mediate p 147and 160-162.

Section Three

Selecting the mediators and organising the Peer Mediation training

Criteria for peer mediator selection

The peer mediators will have a responsible and challenging role to fulfil. For these reasons, it is best if pupils volunteer, and many schools use some kind of a selection process. In selecting from a list of volunteers, care needs to be taken that there is a good gender and ethnicity mix, and that pupils chosen have some of the qualities listed in the Job Description and Person Specification. An initial team of 24 is not too big, and allows for a few to drop out if mediation is not for them. A final team of 16-20 mediators is ideal.

A strong team will support one or two pupils who may have emotional or behavioural difficulties, and who would benefit from this intensive training and responsibility. All the research shows that those who gain the most from Peer Mediation are the mediators themselves, and many pupils who have been through mediation training have been able to use the experience to develop more positive ways of getting attention and influence.

It is a good idea to launch the mediation project with an assembly for all pupils. Ideally this could be led by mediators from a neighbouring school, but if there aren't any, then the video or a live demonstration by members of staff gives the pupils a good idea of what is involved. After the assembly, the Job Description and Application forms can be handed out to pupils who express an interest. Some secondary schools use this as an opportunity for careers education and interview the pupils as if they were applying for a real job.

Some things to consider in the pupil training

During the training it may become apparent that some of the pupils are struggling. If someone wants to leave, then it is important that this is discussed with the rest of the group so that the exit is well managed. If you feel that someone will not be able to mediate after the training, they can still be a part of the team even if they do not do actual mediations.

Those who are not chosen for the training can sometimes feel a little resentful of those who have been chosen. If it is possible, it is a good idea to give them other opportunities to feel useful in school (helping younger children with their reading?).

Peer Mediator

Job Description & Person Specification

Skills

Mediation training will help you to develop skills in listening concentration, creative problem solving, and teamworking. You will learn how to help people to express how they are feeling, and talk about their problem and work out a solution.

You don't have to be good at these things already. Wanting the chance to prove that you can do this well is what matters.

Commitment

You need to be willing to give your time and effort to keep the mediation service running over a long period. This may mean giving up occasional break times on a regular basis.

Qualities

Mediators do not tell people what to do or give advice. They support people in finding their own solutions. They are fair and don't take sides. They can be trusted not to gossip about people's problems.

If you think this is a service you want to help to provide or if you know someone who you think would make a good mediator, please look at the nomination form.

Nomination/Application Form for Peer Mediators

NOMINATION

Please check first with the person you are nominating to be sure that they are willing to be a mediator.

I would like to suggest

name: form:

I think this person would make a good mediator because...

APPLICATION

I would like to apply to be a mediator.

name: form:

I would like the chance to become a mediator because...

I would be a good mediator because...

Section Four

A programme for three days of Peer Mediation training using the video

The three-day training plan can be modified to suit the timetable patterns and constraints of any establishment. However it is important to ensure that all elements of the training are included. The success of the mediation scheme will reflect the quality and thoroughness of the training. Mediators should not begin to use the skills until they have acquired the skills and confidence and when the support structure is in place.

Warm-up and Wind-down Games

Games are the glue that will hold this training together. They are not 'add-ons' to be used as rewards or to fill in a spare five minutes. Frequent use of games will generate an atmosphere of co-operation and fun, and will provide opportunities for both helpful and unhelpful behaviours to emerge which can be discussed as a group. As a rule, it is good idea to name pupils for positive behaviour, but to discuss unhelpful behaviour in more general terms. Some phrases/questions that you may find useful are:

> "I would really like to get on and play this game, but I'm finding that we are not ready to start. What could we do in order to begin the game?"
>
> "I'm noticing that I'm not having as much fun as I was a few minutes ago. Something has changed. What do you think it is? How might we do things differently?"
>
> "During that game I noticed some helpful behaviours and some unhelpful behaviours. Could we have a go-round to share what behaviours you noticed?"
>
> "I would like to thank Stephanie for being so patient during that game. As mediators you will need a lot of patience. Did anyone else notice someone using skills that they will need as a mediator?"

The mediation team will need to be strong and self-directing. Anything you can do to bring this about will pay dividends later when the service is up and running. You should notice a change towards the end of the second day when your role becomes much less directive. At this stage, pupils are able to choose and organise their own games.

The following games are taken from *Let's Mediate*, and have been tried and tested with hundreds of KS1, KS2 and KS3 pupils. They are of course a drop in the ocean of wonderful games that are available. See the bibliography in *Let's Mediate* for more ideas.

What ?	**Why?**	**Pages in *Let's Mediate***
First Introductions	They may not know each other's name. It can be extended as a team-building activity by getting them to repeat it in the same order and timing them. They could then use two balls, or do it in reverse order.	p.27
Signing in	Improves group cohesion and self-esteem	p.28
Dracula	Pupils love it!	p.29
I sit on the hill…	Mixes pupils up. Provides opportunities for choosing people outside of normal friendship groups	p.29
Stand up and change places if…	It mixes pupils up. It can be used to find things in common (e.g. if you have a great grandmother). It energises pupils who have been sitting for a while.	p. 30
I love all my friends…	As the previous game, but with additional fun element because one chair is taken away.	p.31
Co-operative knots	It encourages problem-solving as a team. Safe physical contact strengthens bonds in the group.	p.94

Fives	Pupils love it! Can be done in different languages including the mother tongue of pupils in the group. Can be used to discuss what happens when people are 'out.'	p.95
Spontaneous counting	Helps build awareness of others. Builds a sense of team.	p.96

The Video

The video provides extra reinforcement to your training sessions. It is not intended that the trainees watch the whole video. The scheme indicates which sections are to be shown to pupils. Make sure that the facilitator is very familiar with the video and that the cassette is set ready to show the appropriate section.

A storyboard for the video is provided in section six. The video is divided into the following sections:

Introduction

Conflict situations and the effects on people's lives are shown. Some shots of pupils mediating conflict introduce the ideas to be followed up in the training.

Part 1

The mediation process begins with the pupils introducing themselves. Ways of handling conflict are discussed, drawing out the difference between attacking the opponent and attacking the problem.

Rules for Mediation are discussed.

Part 2

This section of the video illustrates the five steps of Mediation and demonstrates three examples of the process.

Part 3

This section consolidates the training and includes:

spotting deliberate mistakes

understanding some difficulties facing mediators.

Part 4

Young mediators and their teachers discuss their experiences.

Peer Mediation Training: Three Day Programme

Day One

Aims:

- To negotiate an agreed code of conduct, and to generate feelings of pride and belonging in the group.
- To get the group to think about issues of conflict, and relate this work to their own experiences of being in conflict situations, especially the feelings involved.
- To teach active listening skills to use in mediations.
- To introduce the mediation process, and encourage the young people to memorise the promises, rules and steps to the process.

Day one - session one

What ?	How?	Resources
General introduction	Inform them in general terms what they will be doing both over the three days, and what they will do as mediators. The training will be hard work but lots of fun. Dispel any myths (they won't be expected to break up fights!) and give lots of praise. Introduce any visitors who will be helping with the training. Will they be known by their first or second name? It is a real honour and privilege to have been chosen as a mediator. They will find the training useful in all sorts of ways, and they will carry mediation skills with them for the rest of their lives.	
Negotiate a group agreement for a code of conduct	Ask them what rules they would find useful for the training. Are they the same as the rules they use in Circle Time?	

	Agree a visual 'stop talking' signal that anyone in the group can use to bring everyone back together. When someone makes the sign (e.g. hand in the air) everyone else copies and stops talking. What agreement do they want to come to about confidentiality in the group?	
Team-building and communication skills	Circle name games and mixing games: 10-15 minutes Go-round, e.g. 'As a mediator I hope that I will...'	p.39-44
Understanding conflict and strengthening empathy skills	Silent statements. Ask the pupils to stand up and change places if they have been involved in a range of conflict or bullying situations over a specific period of time, e.g. If you have been called a bad name this term, if you have ignored someone who is your friend or not let them play your game since Christmas. Agree beforehand that no one will be 'told off'.	p.140
	The spectrum activity. As above, but use the length of the room to represent a spectrum of 'it's happened a lot' through to 'it hasn't happened to me at all.'	p.140
	How arguments make us feel. Use white board, flip chart, sticky labels, whatever is motivating for your pupils. Try to create an atmosphere of acceptance, stillness and reflection. Discuss how some people respond to conflict by turning outwards (angry outbursts) whilst other turn inwards (sulks, panicky feelings, loneliness). Both are equally valid.	p.142
Being introduced to the mediators on the video	Play the first section of the video discussing the ideas about conflict and showing the mediators introducing themselves.	video Intro
Team-building	Circle games (10-15 minutes).	

Day one - session two

What ?	How?	Resources
Arriving at the ground-rules for the disputants, and the mediator's promises	The ingredients of conflict. Show the three disputes on the video and ask the pupils what they think happens next.	video part 1
	Use the flipchart, artefacts or video to ask the pupils what happens when two disputants attack each other rather than the problem. Which of these behaviours disappear when they attack the problem rather than each other? What then should be the rules of mediation to get disputants to attack the problem rather than each other? Write these up on a flipchart.	video part 1 or p.149
	Discuss in small groups, feed back to the whole group and write up on a flip chart what promises they would require a mediator to make if they were disputants. Watch this being discussed on the video.	video part 1
	Show the five stages of mediation being outlined on the video. Give out the hand-out and briefly discuss each stage with the group.	video part 2 & p.189
	NB. The promises and rules should reflect those shown on the video and written up on p. 160 of Lets Mediate. If the wording varies this is fine, as the pupils need to feel ownership over the process.	
Memorising the ground rules and promises of the mediation process	Ask the pupils what strategies they can think of to help people remember things.	
	Ask them to think of hand signals for each promise / rule to act as aides to memory. An example of this would be a gossiping hand for 'we won't gossip about your problems' or a wagging finger for 'try not to blame.' These hand signals can be used as prompts for rote learning and to get the pupils to test each other. They can also be used on an ongoing basis during mediations as a prompt.	

Recording the ground -rules, promises and stages of the mediation process	Get the pupils to list the problems, rules and stages of the mediation process from the video, from p.160 of *Let's Mediate* or from the flip chart onto index cards. These are small enough to act as prompt cards where necessary without being obtrusive. For best results they can be laminated.	video part 2 p.189 cards/ pens
Team-building	Circle games (10-15 minutes)	

Day one - session three

What ?	How?	Resources
Listening and communications skills	Thirty second pairwork. Use these short activities to emphasise the need to switch off your own need to be listened to during a mediation, and to use good body language for listening.	p.50
	Open and closed questions can be discussed, and games and/or the worksheet can be used to help pupils understand the value of open questions in mediation.	p.53, 181 195, 196
	This handout can be read and discussed with the pupils.	p.194
	Five questions. Use this activity to show the sequence of listening ...remembering ...repeating used in mediation.	p.49-50
	S.A.R.A.H. Present S.A.R.A.(H.) on the flipchart, or give out hand-outs. Discuss why each part of this formula for listening is important. Get them into triads as outlined in the activity and ask the speaker to talk about one of the situations they stood up for in the 'stand up and change places if...' activity they did earlier. The H. of S.A.R.A.H. will not be practised just yet.	H1 p59-60 from no. 7
	Do a go-round as a feedback activity. They could either feed back something their listener did well, how they felt to be really listened to, or how hard it is to listen without making judgements, talking about yourself or giving advice. How is mediating different to chatting with a friend about problems?	
Team-building	Circle games (10-15 minutes)	
Mediation role-play	Show the video clips of KS3, KS2 and KS1 pupils mediating. Get the pupils to make notes about what the main issues in each dispute are. Discuss what they thought about what they saw on the video.	video part 2
	Get the pupils into random groups of 4. A gender mix gets pupils used to working outside of normal friend-ship groups and strengthens the team. Two of the group	

	are mediators and two are disputants. The mediators sit side by side facing the two disputants.	
	The 'What's the Problem?' worksheet can be used to help the two disputants to decide on a coherent and properly thought through conflict. They should be encouraged to avoid the temptation of becoming the disputants from Hell at this stage!	p.190, 192, 193
	The 'Mediator's Prompt Sheet' worksheet can be used to prepare the mediators for the role-play. They should decide who is doing what before they start. They can use their index cards.	p.191
	At the end of the role-play, share with the group what was difficult and what they enjoyed in their role-plays. Can they congratulate anyone on doing very well?	
	Give out handouts H8 and 9 and ask the pupils to read it several times at home for home-work.	H. 8 & 9
Rounding off	Circle activity for fun and team-building, e.g. Number games. Go-round, 'What I most enjoyed today was…'	p.95

Day Two

Aims:

- To continue to build a sense of team and self-determination in the group.
- To consolidate the mediation process through demonstrations and practice.
- To begin the process of assessing the mediators.
- To begin laying the foundations of safety and good practice guidelines for the mediators.

Day two - session one

What ?	How?	Resources
Teambuilding and affirmation work	Various Circle Time games, and some reflection on what we did well yesterday, and what we need to do today.	
Avoiding mistakes	Show the video footage of Hilary mediating between Big Grey and Little Red. Stop the video as indicated, and ask the pupils to say what was done wrong, and what needs to happen next. This could be done live in the classroom with one of the trainers and two pupils role-playing. It works well as a quiz show with pupils pressing imaginary buzzers to stop the action and say what was done wrong etc.	video part 3
Mediation role-play	As Day One Session Three Pupils will need to play both a disputant and a mediator several times before they feel confident in the process. Choose one of the groups to demonstrate (voluntarily!) in front of the others. Stop them if they make a mistake and ask them what they need to do next. The others can help if the mediators are stuck.	
Peer review	Get the mediators into groups of six (by now they should be confident about working in mixed gender groups). In each group there are two mediators, two disputants, and two observers.	

	Each observer assesses the speaking and listening skills of one of the mediators in a role-play, using the hand-outs. At the end of the role-play the observers share what they have put on the assessment sheets with the mediators. Swap roles in the group until everyone has been assessed. If the pupils are not used to this form of assessment, time will need to be spent helping them understand the importance of being both positive and honest.	H. 5 & 6
Team-building	Circle games (10-15 minutes).	

Day two - session two

What ?	How?	Resources
A team challenge to assess the pupils' readiness to work together as a team	These activities are best done in the hall or outside. A brief warm-up activity, e.g. Sharks. Set the team an 'outward bound' type challenge. An example is giving them four hoops to get across a 'swamp' that is too long for them to use the hoops as stepping-stones. Eventually someone will realise that they can all go across together if the rear hoop keeps getting passed forward to the front. Try not to intervene or make suggestions, even if it looks like you will still be there by Christmas! Take a notepad and record a comment about each pupil's contribution to the team to feed back at the end. If things have not progressed after about 30 minutes you could silently place the talking object in the middle of a circle of chairs. During the feedback ask them each to name someone who acted as a good team-member. Stress the positive, and remind them that they will need to function as a strong team if their mediation service is to be successful.	 p.88

Day two - session three

What ?	How?	Resources
Whole-group mediation	Do a 'fish-bowl' role-play with two volunteer mediators to start, and others coming in to take over at particular points. If this is done in a big circle no one has their back to anyone else, and everyone can hear. Discuss the issues that come out as a whole group.	
Setting up the service	What ifs... This can be done by getting pupils in groups to write down three 'What if's' on a sheet of paper (What if your sister expects you to be on her side? What if one of the disputants starts to cry?) The sheets are then circulated amongst the other groups and they write suggestions for each other onto the sheets. This is followed by whole-group discussion.	p. 174-180
	Instead of, or in addition to this, the video can be shown and stopped as indicated for pupils to give their ideas.	video part 3
	At this point it is vital to stress the following points. The hand-out H 7 should be copied for all children so that they have a written record. Ideally it should be included in their mediation hand-book: • There is never any confidentiality from teachers. Mediators don't gossip to other pupils, but they do tell their mediation co-ordinator about what they are mediating. • Mediators do not mediate problems from home. • Where there is anything that is a serious infringement of school rules (violence, drugs, racism, weapons) a teacher must be told immediately and the mediation stopped. • They must not touch the disputants, either to break up a fight or to comfort them when they are upset. • A teacher or supervisor will always be within easy reach when they are mediating.	H. 7
Rounding off	Circle games chosen by the group.	

Day Three

Aims:

- To strengthen feelings of self-determination in the group.
- To assess pupils's ability to mediate.
- To establish the Peer Mediation scheme.

Day three - session one

What ?	**How?**	**Resources**
Warm-up session	Circle games chosen by the group	
Assessment of mediation skills	Pupils assess their peers' mediation skills as in Day Two. Staff use this as a final opportunity to assess whether all pupils are ready to mediate.	H2, 3, & 4

Day three - sessions two and three

What ?	How?	Resources
Use of games as before		
Designing the service	Small groups take responsibility for various aspects for setting up the service, e.g. creating a rota, designing posters, etc. Suggested groups: • Practicalities group (when, where, badges, rota). • Assembly group. • Publicity group (posters, letters to parents, media). • Mediators handbook group (names of mediators, what we do/don't mediate, promises and rules, what to do if... mediators' safety rules). Each group is encouraged to designate roles for each team member and create an action-plan and time-scale. The groups will create options for the whole-group, but final decisions will need to be decided by everyone.	167 - 168 174 - 176 H.10. 11, & 12 work on computers
Consultation with senior managers	Pupils consult with the Head or a Deputy to establish the viability of their ideas for running the service.	
Ending and celebration of achievements	Go-rounds where peers affirm each other's contribution to the team, and games.	

On-going training and support for the peer mediators

It is important to celebrate the achievements of the mediators when the training is complete. An example of a certificate is included.

Being a mediation co-ordinator does take time! Mediators will need to meet weekly as a team with their mediation teacher to discuss what they have been mediating, to let off steam, and to pool ideas for moving forward with difficult cases. If the service is not being used, then weekly meetings will need to focus on the reasons why and on trouble-shooting. Support and evaluation are essential and must be planned within the programme.

SARAH

Stop Talking and ***Switch off*** your own need to be listened to. Check that your body language ***shows*** that you are listening.

Actively listen to what your speaker is saying. Listen as if your life depends on it, and only ***ask*** questions if you are unclear about something, to find out how they are feeling or if they stop talking. Let them decide what they want to talk about.

Repeat a summary of what you heard them say. Be as accurate as possible. Make sure that you ***reflect*** back to them how they said they were feeling. Your speaker should appreciate the fact that you were really listening to them, and you know how they were feeling.

Accept what they are saying even if you think that they are wrong. Show your ***acceptance*** that they have the right to feel any way they please. Remember: feelings are facts. ***Act*** with empathy.

Help them to think of ways forward. Your listening to them will have helped them to be more positive. Make sure that you don't give them advice, either directly or indirectly. Only they know what they need. The aim is to put people back in charge of their own life.

H 1

Mediation Training — Peer Assessment

Name of Mediator

Name of Assessor

The Mediation Process	Can't do this yet	Need a lot more practise	Getting better at this	Can do this	Do this well
Know how to put people at ease at the beginning of the mediation					
Is able to be warm and welcoming to the disputants					
Can remember both sets of ground rules (for mediators and disputants)					
Can remind people firmly but kindly to keep the ground rules					
Can remember the steps of the mediation process (the way it works) in the right order					
Can treat both people the same H 2					

Mediation Training — Peer Assessment

Name of Mediator

Name of Assessor

The Mediation Process (Cont 1)	**Can't do this yet**	**Need a lot more practise**	**Getting better at this**	**Can do this**	**Do this well**
Can help the disputants to understand each others feelings without blaming					
Can encourage the two disputants to brainstorm a fair list of suggestions for solving problem					
Can make sure that any offers or suggestions about how to solve the problem are fair and not one-sided					
Can repeat back all the suggestions that have been made					
Can manage not to give advice or tell people what they should do H 3					

Mediation Training — Peer Assessment

Name of Mediator

Name of Assessor

The Mediation Process (Cont 2)	Can't do this yet	Need a lot more practise	Getting better at this	Can do this	Do this well
Makes sure both people are completely happy with the suggest-ions chosen for the solution					
Can help both people to decide what to do next time to prevent the same thing from happening again					
Remembers to let them know that they can come back to check if their agreement is working or to make changes to it H 4					

Mediation Training — Peer Assessment

Name of Mediator

Name of Assessor

Listening	Can't do this yet	Need a lot more practise	Getting better at this	Can do this	Do this well
Can make good eye contact					
Can stay calm and still					
Can sit in an open and relaxed way when listening					
Give full attention to listening					
Can listen without interrupting or asking too many questions					
Can reflect back feelings and what was said accurately					
Can accept the person's point of view and feelings					
Can listen in an understanding and sympathetic way H 5					

Mediation Training — Peer Assessment

Name of Mediator

Name of Assessor

Speaking	Can't do this yet	Need a lot more practise	Getting better at this	Can do this	Do this well
Can use open questions and ways of helping people to open up and talk					
Can remember to ask about each person's feelings					
Doesn't take over by talking too much or asking too many questions					
Can keep a calm and friendly tone of voice					
Remembers to congratulate both people if they manage to come to an agreement H 6					

Mediators' Safety Rules

√ There is never any confidentiality from teachers. Mediators don't gossip to other pupils, but they do tell their mediation teacher about what they are mediating.

√ Mediators do not mediate problems from home.

√ Where there is anything that is against school rules (violence, drugs, racism, weapons) a teacher must be told immediately and the mediation stopped.

√ Mediators must not touch the disputants, either to break up a fight or to comfort them when they are upset.

√ A teacher or supervisor will always be within easy reach when mediators are mediating.

H 7

The Mediators Script

Do say things like...

Thank you for both coming.

This is a really good start. It means that you would both like to sort things out.

It's a hopeful sign that we might arrive at a solution.

We're here to help you both. Can we remind you about the things we'll be doing.

First of all, as mediators, we...
won't take sides,
won't suggest solutions,
will keep what you say a secret unless you tell us something that might be dangerous or harmful to other people or yourself, and will help you to keep to the rules of mediation, which are...

1. give each other time to speak without interrupting,
2. speak about each other without swearing or name calling,
3. speak about the problem as it affects you
4. try not to accuse other people.

Would one of you like to go first?

Thank you for being patient and waiting for your turn to speak.

(Name)... can you tell me about the problem from your point of view? How is it affecting you?

So let me just check that I have got this right...

If I can be clear about this...

Could you just explain a little more about... so that I can be sure I understand?

Thank you (name)

H8

Try not to say things like...

Right, we're here to sort this out and get to the bottom of things.

Right, just as well you two have turned up.

I don't know what we're going to do with you.

You again (name)...?

You've both been very silly (stupid, badly behaved, irresponsible etc.)

What have you got to say for yourselves then?

Why did you...?

You should have...

Can't you understand that...?

You should have...

You know very well that you...

In my opinion...

What I suggest you do is...

How would you like it?

I'm very disappointed in you.

The Mediators Script

Try to say things like...(after first person has finished speaking)

Thank you (name) and thank you (second name) or waiting patiently for your turn. Will you explain the problem from your point of view now and say how it affects you?

So let me just check that I've got this right... What you're saying is... etc.

(Name)... has said she/he feels... (angry/sad, etc.) when you... Can you see how she/her might be feeling... (angry/sad)?

Can you see how she/he would be feeling that? (*If response is "yes BUT..." interrupt the BUT with,* "Right. So you can understand that.") Would you just tell (name)... that?

I wonder if you could just let (name) know that?

We know you are (hurt/upset/angry). Can you put that aside for a moment and...

Thank you for that (name). We're at a stage where we can look at ideas to solve this now. We need some suggestions from each of you.

Let's look at what you can offer. *(accept ALL)* (Name) has offered to..., what will you offer?

We'll come on to requests in a minute. What can you offer? Now let's look at any requests you might have.

(evaluating suggestions) We've got some good suggestions here. Would you like to say which of these you think would work or which you would like to choose to start with?

Good, we have an agreement. How would you like to seal this agreement?

Congratulations. Very well done both of you. Thank you both. Would you like to come back together to check how you're doing?

Next meeting to evaluate. "I'm noticing that... hearing that... are you comfortable with that?"

H9

Try not to say things like…

Can't you see that she/he's upset?

What would your…mum…dad…teacher… say if they knew?

Well, you shouldn't have done that should you?

How would you feel if someone did that to you?

Now don't be silly.

Nobody's going to hurt you.

There's nothing to worry about.

Will you just stop getting so worked up?

I just can't see what all the fuss is about.

Well, that's nothing to worry about.

I know someone who did the same thing and they said…

I've had that happen to me and…

My advice to you would be to…

Now say you're sorry.

Now both of you shake hands… and no hard feelings.

Now both of you make friends.

Now go away and both of you be nice to each other.

I don't want to see you in here again.

H9 continued

Working Group Tasks

Name of group

People in the group

Name	Task	Completed by
H 10		

Weekly Mediation Rota

Day	Date	Mediators	Place	Done
Monday				
Tuesday				
Wednesday				
Thursday				
Friday				

Days or times when people are not free - duty swaps	Day	Time
H11		

A list of the trained mediators in our school

These are the members of staff who are involved with the service....

H 12

Peer Mediation

This is to certify that

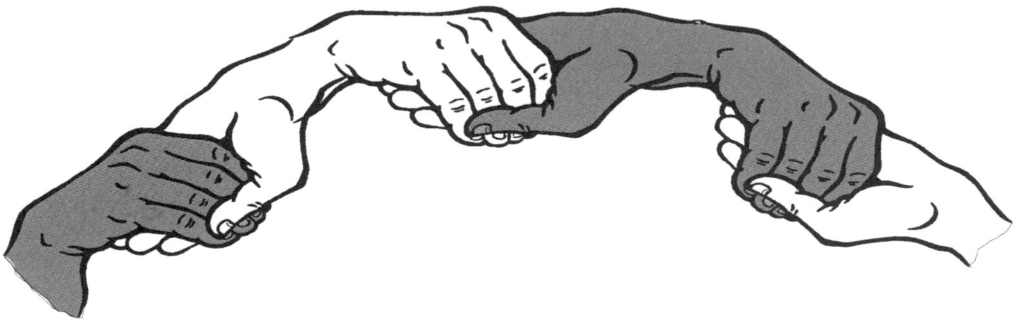

has participated in three days of
Peer Mediation Training
and has been selected as a
School Mediator

Signed **Date**

Section Five

Video storyboard

Mediation training for infant, junior and secondary pupils.

Video based on the work of Catalyst Consultancy.

Introduction
Reasons for conflict and how they can affect our lives are explained . Different scenes of pupils playing in school playgrounds are shown. Scenes of pupils in conflict are shown. Scenes of pupils as peer mediators are shown illustrating what happens in the mediation process.

PART ONE: The Mediation Process

Hilary introduces herself and explains why the pupils are there – to train as peer mediators. The pupils, from KS1, KS2 and KS3, introduce themselves, giving their name, age and why they want to be a peer mediator for their school.

Scenes of pupils in playground disputes are shown. Hilary asks the prospective mediators what happens during the conflict – argue, blaming, not listening, anger, violence, not co-operating, upset, name calling, etc.. Hilary illustrates what would happen if the disputants attacked the problem instead of each other. With the exception of angry and upset, the problem would disappear. It is, therefore, 'feelings' that have to be resolved.

Mediation
Hilary and the pupils discuss what rules should be laid down for the mediation process in order for it to work.

Rules for mediation
Disputants should:

- Wait their turn to speak
- Speak with respect at all times
- Don't blame the other person.

Mediators promises

- I won't gossip
- I won't take sides
- I won't tell you what to do.

PART TWO: Five Steps of Mediation

Step 1 Introduction

The mediators give their names and find out if mediation is wanted.
KS1M asks: "Would you like us to sort out your problem?"
The mediator gains their agreement to stick to the rules.
KS3M asks: "Are you clear about the rules?"

Step 2 Listening

The mediator asks what the problem is and listens to each of them.
KS3M asks: "Can you tell us your side of the story?"

Step 3 Acknowledgement

The mediator summarises the problem for each of them and asks them if then can acknowledge each other's feelings.

Step 4 Suggestions

The mediator asks them to think how they can sort it out.
KS2M asks: "What do you think you could do to solve this problem?"

Step 5 Agreement

The mediator helps them come to an agreement.
KS2M asks: Do you agree to this?
The mediator supports them to think of the future.
KS2M asks: Would you like to be friends?

Mediation 1 (Saba and Jennifer)

KS3 Wasim and Selma

Wasim welcomes them.

Selma gives promises and rules.

Wasim asks Saba to say her side of the story.

The argument is about Tasnim who is new to the school. Saba decided that she could hang around in her gang for a few days. Saba liked her and got to know her. Jennifer, who is Saba's best friend, spread rumours that Saba was 'deffing her out' since Tasnim started the school.

Wasim summarises what Saba has said and asks for Jennifer's side of the story.

Jennifer says that she was getting upset because Saba is leaving her out, and they are supposed to be best friends.

Wasim summarises what Jennifer has said and asks Saba if she can see Jennifer's point of view.

Saba says that she can see Jennifer's point of view and does want to be her friend, but she also wants to be friends with Tasnim.

Selma asks Jennifer if she can understand what Saba is saying.

Jennifer says that she can understand what Saba is saying, and that she now wants to move on and forget about the argument. She offers to get to know Tasnim better.

Wasim asks them if they can think of any solutions.

Saba suggests that they all hang around together.

Jennifer agrees to get to know Tasnim better.

Wasim asks if they are clear about their agreement and invites them to 'shake on it'.

Mediation 2 (Tasnim and Shamrez)

KS2 Nosheen and Kamal

Nosheen welcomes them and gives promises. Kamal gives them their rules.

Nosheen asks if they agree to keep them.

Nosheen asks who wants to go first.

Tasnim says she would like to start and then gives her side of the story.

She was in the middle of a brilliant pass in football when Shamrez got in the way. He didn't appear to care or to respect the game that was going on.

Shamrez interrupts and says that what she is saying is unfair.

Nosheen reminds him to keep to the rules.

He agrees.

Tasnim continues, saying that Shamrez didn't say sorry and just walked off.

Nosheen summarises what Tasnim has said and asks Shamrez for his side of the story.

Shamrez says that he was walking across the game to go and see his friend when he got in the way of Tasnim's pass. Tasnim called him a pain in the neck.

Kamal summarises what Shamrez has just said and asks Tasnim how she is feeling.

Tasnim says she is feeling upset, angry and disappointed because her game is ruined.

Kamal asks Shamrez if he can understand Tasnim's feelings.

Shamrez says yes.

Nosheen asks Shamrez how he is feeling.

Shamrez says he is feeling upset because Tasnim is calling him a pain in the neck.

Nosheen asks Tasnim if she can understand Sahmrez's feelings.

Tasnim says yes.

Nosheen asks both of them what they can think of to solve the problem.

Shamrez offers to not get in the way of her game in future.

Tasnim says that next time she won't call him a pain in the neck.

Kamal asks them if the both agree and if they want to be friends.

They say yes to both.

Nosheen asks them if they want to shake hands and they do.

Mediation 3 (Tom and Jo)

KS 1 Christie and Kate

Tom and Jo are play-fighting Power Rangers. Jo hurt Tom and laughs.
Tom tells him not to laugh and they argue about whether it was on purpose.
The mediators introduce themselves and ask if they would like to be mediated.
They say yes.
Christie tells them the two mediator's promises which are to be fair and not to boss them around.
Kate tells them their rules, which are to speak one at a time and to speak nicely to each other.
Kate asks them if they agree to the rules.
They do.
Christie asks Tom to say his side of the story.
Tom says that they were playing Power Rangers when Jo kicked him and started laughing.
Christie summarises.
Kate asks Jo for his side of the story.
Jo says that he did kick him, but he didn't mean to laugh.
Kate summarises.
Christie asks what they can do about this in future.
Jo says he will be more careful and they could play a less rough game.
Tom says they could play a different game and say sorry.

PART THREE: Consolidation of the Mediation Process

Spotting the Deliberate Mistakes

Hilary mediates between Big Grey and Little Red and makes a series of mistakes.

1. Hilary forgets to say the third rule, which is that Big Grey and Little Red must tell their side of the story without blame.

Big Grey says his side of the story.

2. Hilary forgets to repeat/summarise what Big Grey says.

Little Red says her side of the story.

3. Hilary makes a judgement about whether Little Red should have been in the forest on her own, and therefore takes sides.
   Big Grey and Little Red acknowledge each other's feelings.

4. Hilary begins to offer a solution.

What if...?

The practicalities of setting up a mediation service.

What if...

...they break the rules

- remind them of the rules
- give them three warnings then stop the mediation

...they were shy

- take them to separate rooms
- stop the mediation
- ask them open questions to help them feel more comfortable

...they had language difficulties

- get someone to translate

...they want to fight

- call off the mediation and get a teacher
- offer to mediate when they have calmed down

...your brother/sister come for mediation

- ask someone else to mediate

...they start to cry

- hand them a tissue - it's OK to cry.

PART FOUR: Mediation, our experiences

The Mediators

KS2 mediators talk about their service:

We mediate in the library at dinnertimes and playtimes.
We have a rota.
I did a mediation about football.
I did a mediation about name-calling.

KS3 mediators talk about their service:

We mediate in the community room at lunchtimes and breaktimes.
People know who the mediators are because we wear mediators' caps.
We advertised our service through posters and an assembly.
Mediation has made me more confident and made me a very good listener.
I feel good that I can help other people with their problems.

The Teachers

The Headteacher at Washwood Heath C.J.C. talks about why he supports Peer Mediation in his school:

It's essential that students are involved in the process of resolving difficulties in school.

It's important that schools work together to do this work so that pupils can extend their skills at secondary level.

Staff training takes place regularly with teachers from across the consortium of schools being trained over two days.

Washwood Heath is now benefiting from a good number of pupils arriving with mediation skills from their primary schools.

In order to sustain the programme Y7 tutors are trained each year to ensure a rolling programme, with most teachers in the school able to support the work both through PSHE and other areas of the curriculum.

At the end of each term, training is offered to Y7 mediators.

The benefits of mediation include a high level of confidence for the mediators themselves which improves their learning, and a support service for new pupils coming in to the school.

Key Stages 1 and 2

A KS1 teacher talks about basic mediation skills-training at KS1:

It usually takes the form of Circle Time.
It develops speaking and listening skills and turn-taking/co-operation.
Mediation becomes more formal at KS2 and builds on work done in KS1.

A KS2 teacher talks about mediation at KS2:

It develops confidence and self-esteem.
The pupils develop a sense of responsibility and fairness.
Pupils with problems open up more to their peers and talk more freely.
They learn to resolve problems through peaceful means.

A bibliography is provided in *Let's Mediate*

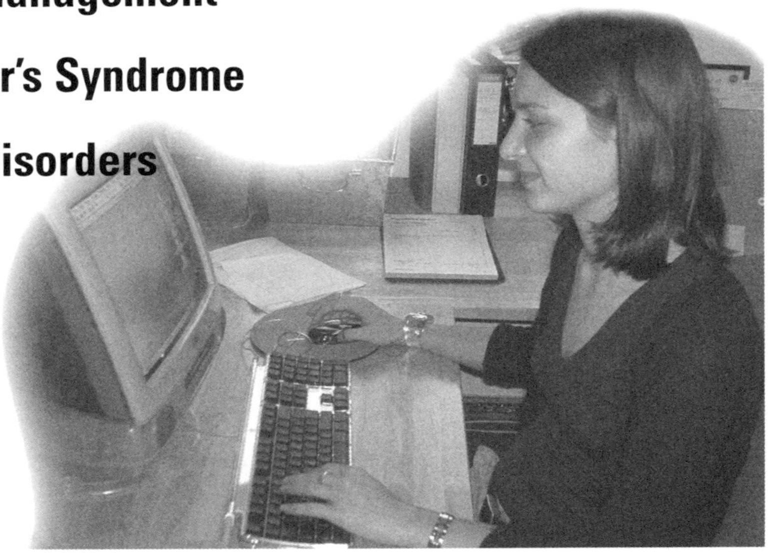